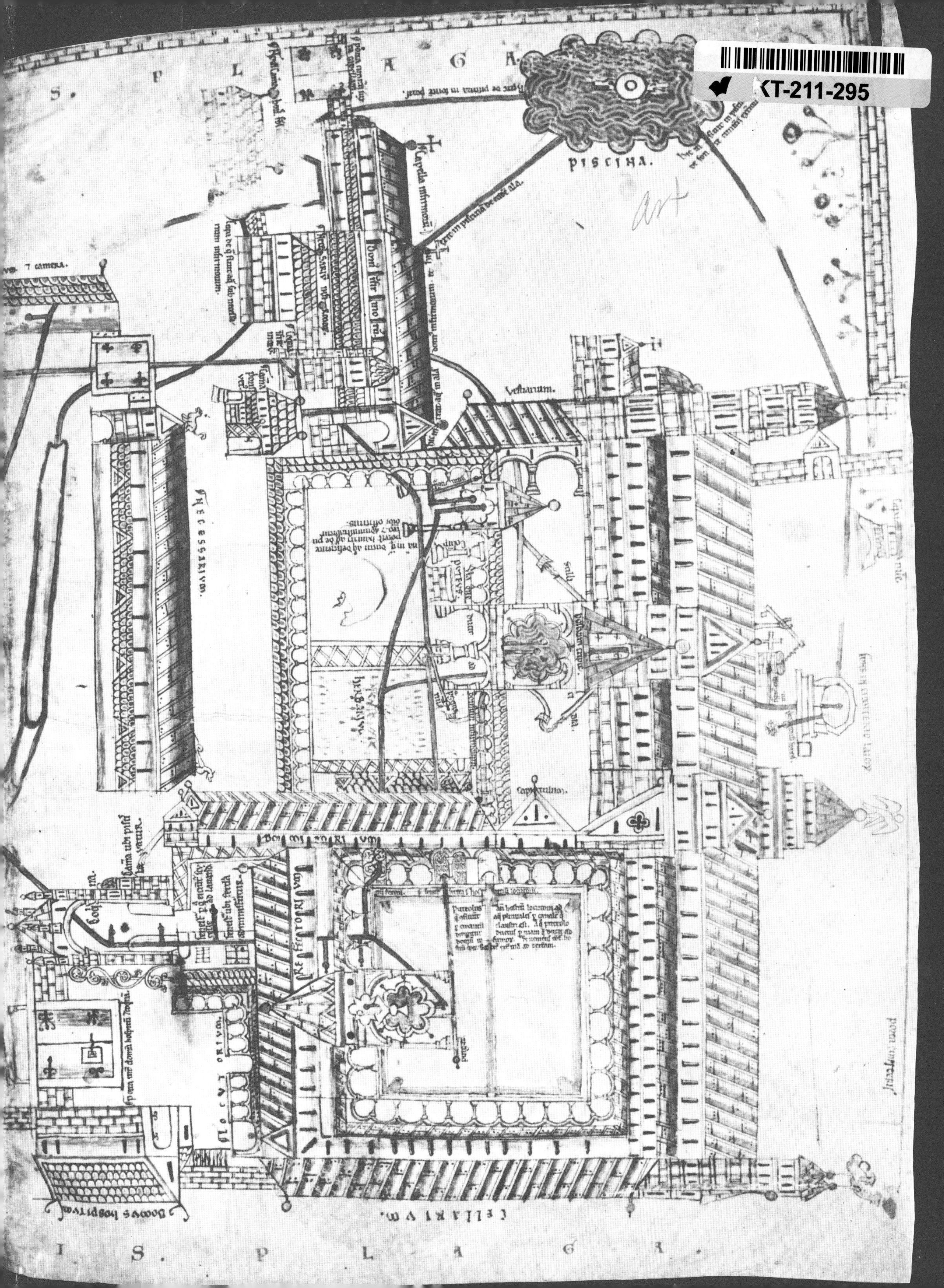
PISCINA.
NECESSARIUM.
Vestiarium.
Capitulum
CELLARIVM.

From the library of
John Stoye (1917-2016)

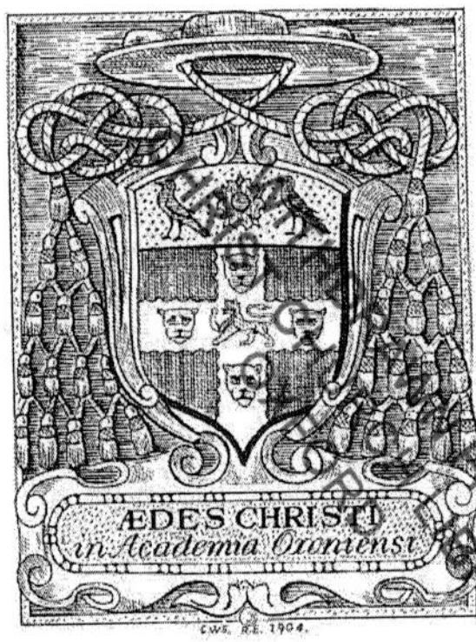

Historian and Author
Christ Church, m.1936
Dixon Scholar 1946